Jack Johnson
ANTHOLOGY

CONTENTS

Piano/Vocal arrangements by John Nicholas
Additional arranging by Doug Pew and Charles Ancheta

Cherry Lane Music Company
Director of Publications/Project Editor: Mark Phillips
Publications Coordinator: Gabrielle Fastman

ISBN 1-57560-851-0

Visit our website at www.cherrylane.com

Banana Pancakes

Words and Music by
Jack Johnson

Ain't no need, ain't no need. Mm, mm,— mm, mm.

Can't you see, can't you see?——

Rain all day and I don't mind.— But the

tel - e - phone's sing - ing, ring - ing. It's too ear - ly; don't pick it up.——

4

Wake up slow. _____ But, ba - by, you

Ain't no need, ain't no need.

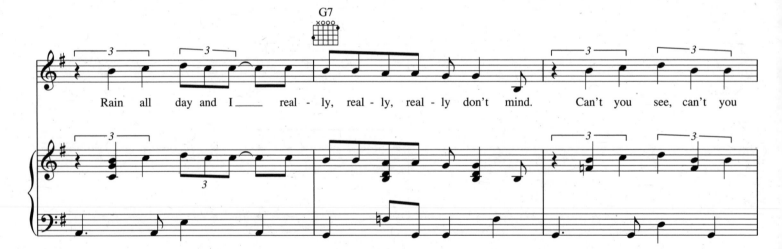

Rain all day and I ___ real - ly, real - ly, real - ly don't mind. Can't you see, can't you

see? We've got to wake up slow. _____

Belle

Words and Music by
Jack Johnson

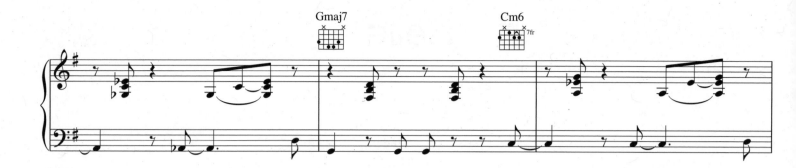

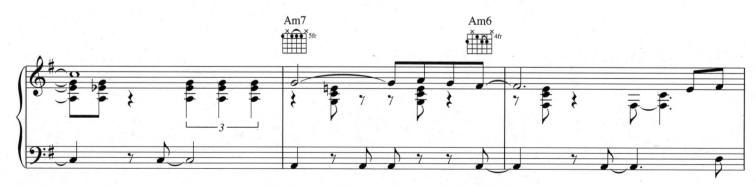

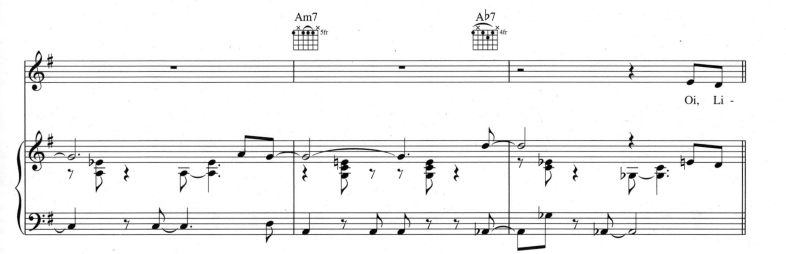

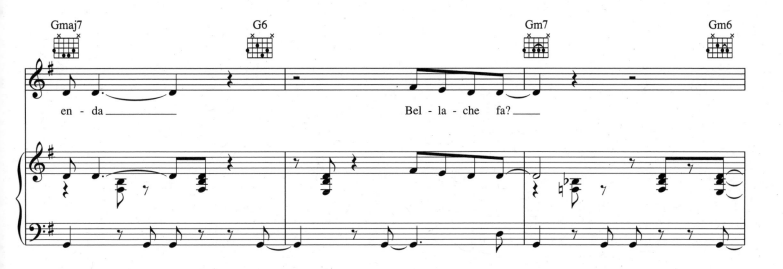

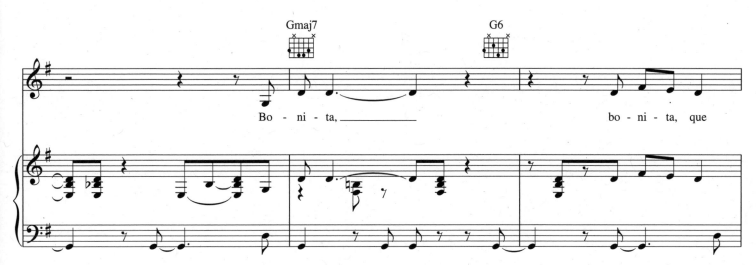

tal? But belle, je ne com - prends __ pas __ fran - çais. So you'll have to speak to me some oth - er way.

10

Better Together

Words and Music by
Jack Johnson

Mm, ___ it's al - ways bet - ter when we're to - geth - er.
Yeah, ___ it's al - ways bet - ter when we're to - geth - er.

Yeah, ___ we look at the stars when we're to - geth - er. }
Mm, ___ we're some - where in be - tween to - geth - er. }

Well, ___ it's al - ways bet - ter when we're to - geth - er.

Yeah, ___ it's al - ways bet - ter when we're to - geth - er. ___

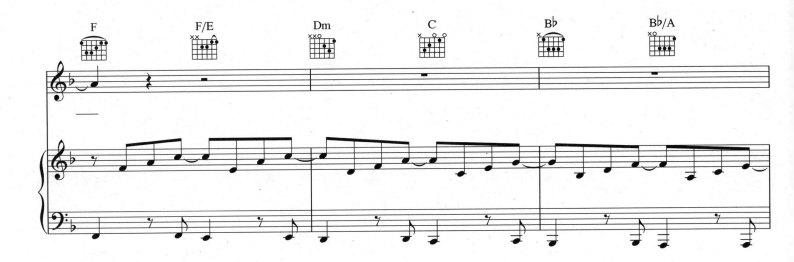

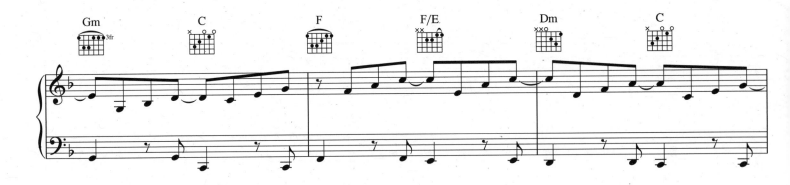

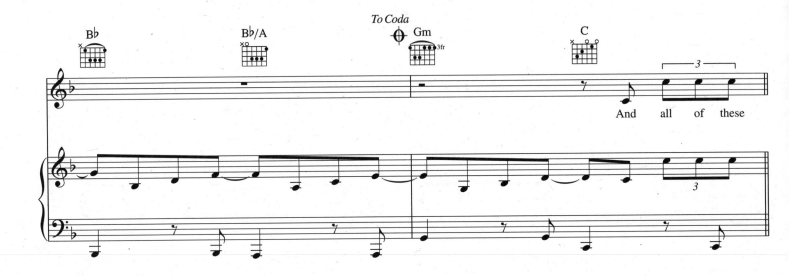

And all of these

mo - ments just might find a way in - to my dreams ___ to - night, ___ but I

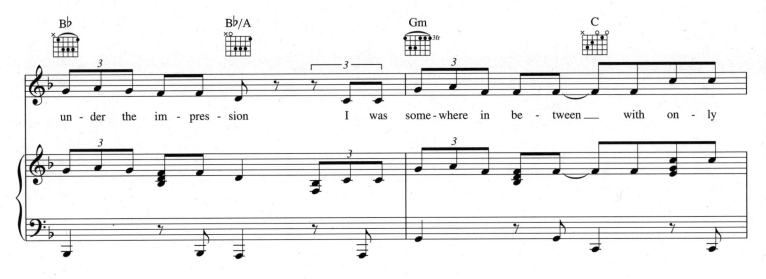

un - der the im - pres - sion I was some - where in be - tween ___ with on - ly

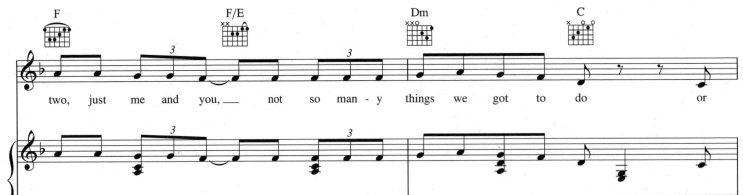

two, just me and you, ___ not so man - y things we got to do or

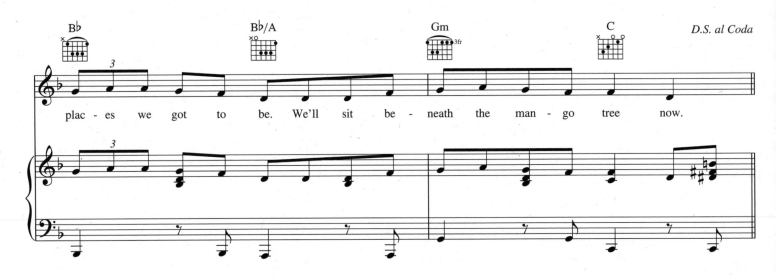

D.S. al Coda

plac - es we got to be. We'll sit be - neath the man - go tree now.

I be - lieve in mem - o -

ries; they look so, so pret-ty when I sleep.___ Hey, now and,___

___ and when I wake ___ up, ___ you look so pret-ty sleep-ing next to

me. But there is ___ not e-nough time.___ And there is no,___

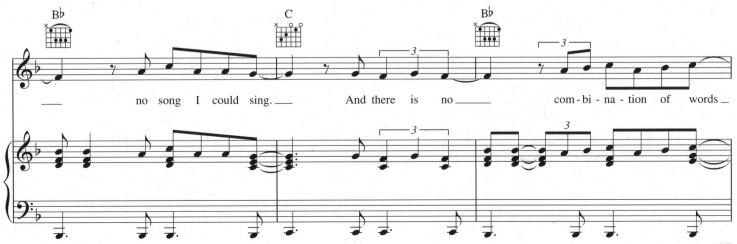

___ no song I could sing.___ And there is no ___ com-bi-na-tion of words___

I could say, __ but I will still tell you one thing: __ We're bet-ter to-geth - er. __

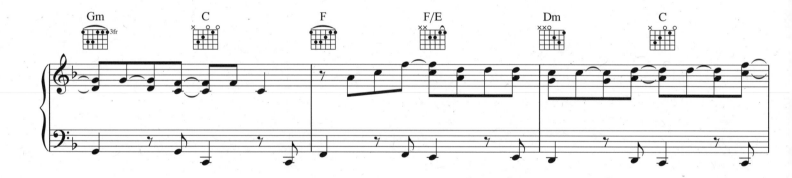

18

Breakdown

Words and Music by
Jack Johnson, Dan Nakamura
and Paul Huston

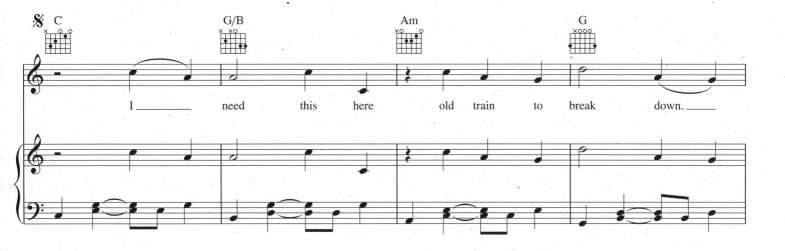

I _____ need this here old train to break down. _____

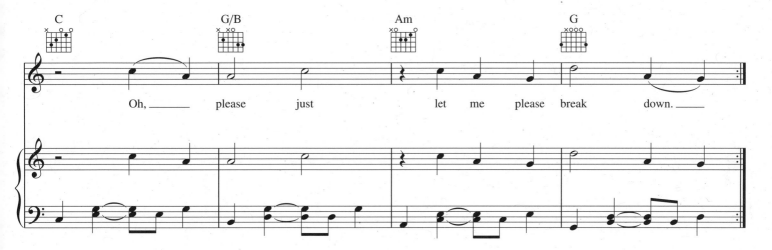

Oh, _____ please just let me please break down. _____

I _____ need this here old train to break down. _____

To Coda ⊕

Oh, _____ please just let me please break down. _____

I wan-na break on down. _____ But I can't stop now. _____

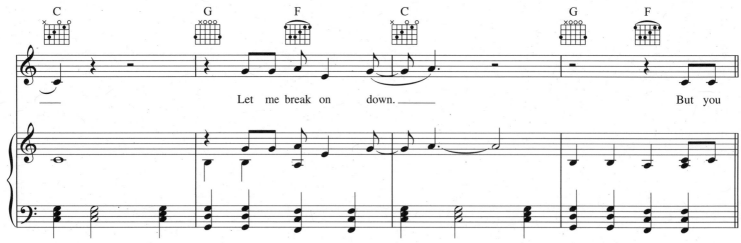

Let me break on down. _____ But you

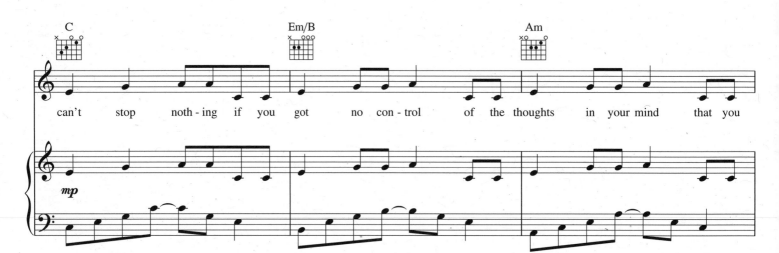

can't stop noth-ing if you got no con-trol of the thoughts in your mind that you

kept in, you know. You don't know noth-ing but you don't need to know. The

wis-dom's in the trees, not the glass win - dows. You can't stop wish-ing if you

don't let go the things that you find and you lose and you know. You

keep on roll-ing, put the mo-ment on hold. The frames too bright so put the

D.S. (no repeat) al Coda

blinds down low. And...

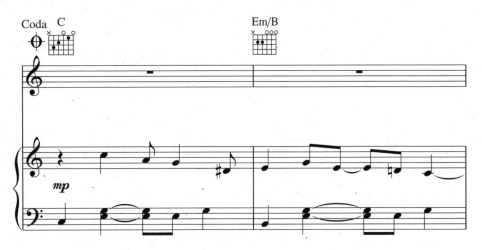

I wan - na break on   down. _____

But   I   can't   stop   now. _

Bubble Toes

Words and Music by
Jack Johnson

I'll re - mem - ber when ___ you and me, ___ mm, ___ how we used to be ___ just good friends. Would - n't give me none, ___ but all I want - ed ___ was some.

She's got-ta whole lot-ta rea - sons. She can't think of a

sin-gle one __ that can jus-ti-fy __ leav - ing. And he got none, __ but he thinks __ he got so man-y prob-

lems. Man, he got too much time __ to waste. __

His dreams are like __ com - mer - cials, but __ her dreams __

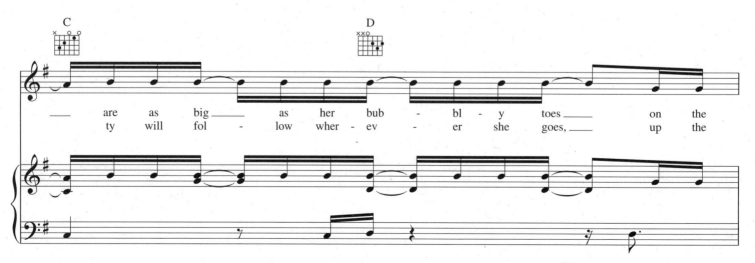

feet of a queen ___ of the hearts ___ of the cards, ___ She'll
hill in the back ___ of her house ___ in the wood. ___

feet are in - fest - ed with tar ___ balls and... } La, da, da, da, da, ___ da.
love me for - ev - er, I know ___ she...

La, da, da, da, ___ da, da, ___ da. La, da, da, da, da, ___ da.

To Coda II

To Coda I

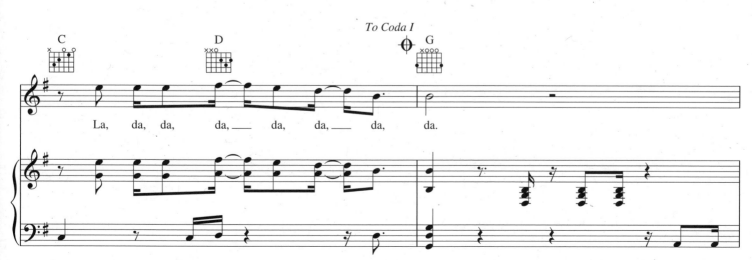

La, da, da, da, ___ da, da, ___ da, da.

Well,

I was eat-ing lunch at the D. L. G.__ when this lit-tle girl came__ and she sat next to me.

Nev-er seen no-bod-y move the way she did.__ Well, she did and she does and she'll do it a-gain.__ When you

move like a jel-ly-fish, rhy-thm don't mean noth-ing. You go with the flow; you don't__ stop.

Move like a jel - ly - fish, rhy - thm is noth - ing. You go with the flow; you don't_ stop. Mm._

D.S. al Coda I

It's as

Coda I

da.

If

you would on - ly lis - ten, you might just real - ize what you're miss - ing. You're miss - ing me._

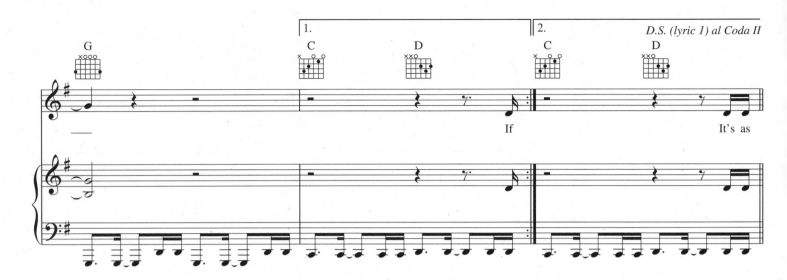

If

It's as

La, da, da, da, __ da, da, __ da. La, da, da, da, da, __ da.

La, da, da, da, __ da, da, __ da. La, da, da, da, da, __ da.

La, da, da, da, __ da, da, __ da, da.

Constellations

Words and Music by
Jack Johnson

The light was leav-ing; in the west it was blue.___ The

chil - dren's laugh - ter___ sang,___ skip-ping just like the

*Recorded a half step higher.

stones they threw. __ Their voic - es ech - oed a - cross the waves. __

__ It's get - ting late. _____

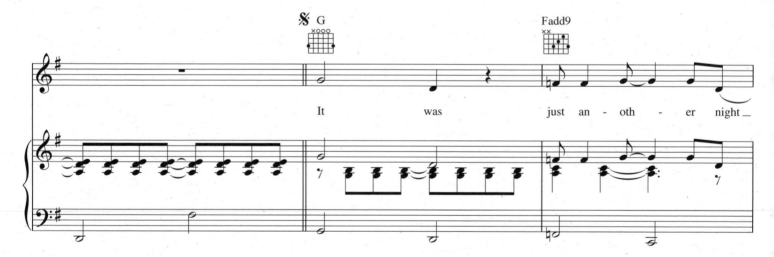

It was just an - oth - er night __

__ with the sun - set and __ a _____ moon - rise

The west winds___ of - ten last too long, ___ and when they calm down,

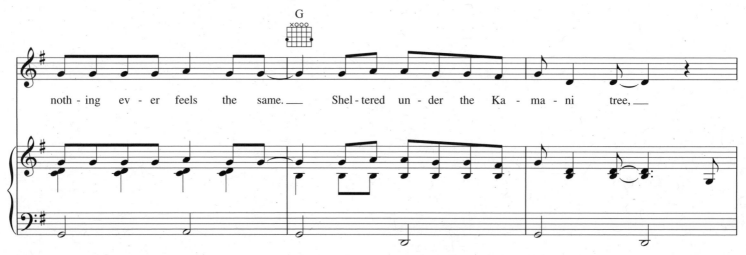

noth - ing ev - er feels the same. ___ Shel - tered un - der the Ka - ma - ni tree, ___

waiting for the pass - ing ___ rain. ___ Clouds keep mov - ing to un -

cov - er the sea ___ of stars a - bove us, chas - ing the day a - way ___

___ to find the sto - ries that we some - times need. ___ Lis - ten close e - nough, ___

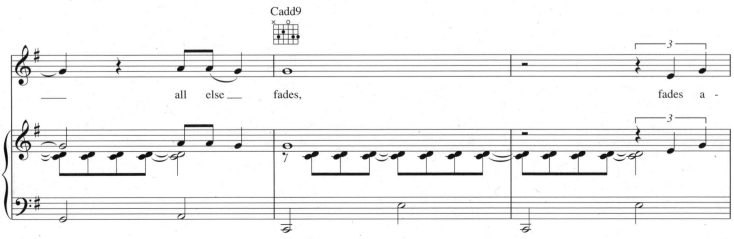

___ all else ___ fades, fades a -

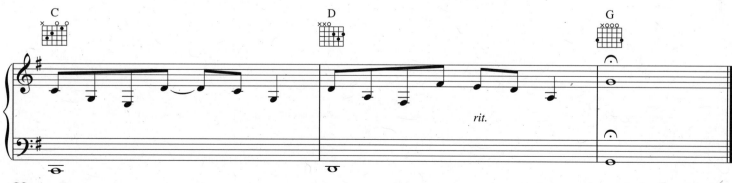

Cookie Jar

Words and Music by
Jack Johnson

F#m ... C#m

been kill - ing me ev - er since it be - gun. You
I just point my cam - 'ra at what the peo - ple want to see. Man, it's a

B ... C#m

can't blame me _____ 'cause I'm _____ too young." _____
two - way mir - ror and you can't _____ blame me." _____

F#m ... C#m ... B ... C#m

"You
"You

F#m ... C#m

can't blame me. _____ Sure, the kill - er was my son, but I
can't blame me," _____ says the sing - er of the song or the

B   C#m

did - n't teach him _____ to pull the trig - ger of the gun. It's the
mak - er of the mov - ie which he based his life on. "It's

1.
F#m   C#m   B   C#m

kill - ing on his T - V screen. _ You can't blame me; it's the im - ag - es he's _ seen." _____

F#m   C#m   B   C#m

_____ "Well, _____ you

2.
F#m   C#m

on - ly en - ter - tain - ment, and as an - y - one can see, it's

smoke ma - chines and make - up. Man, you can't fool me."

It was

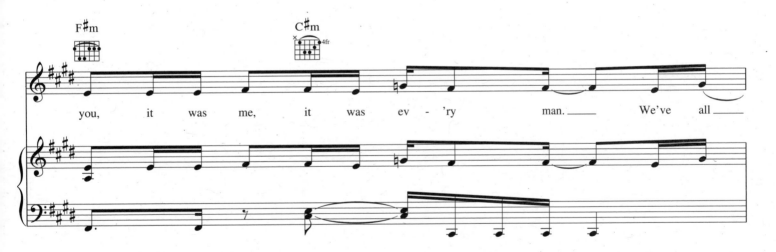

you, it was me, it was ev - 'ry man. We've all

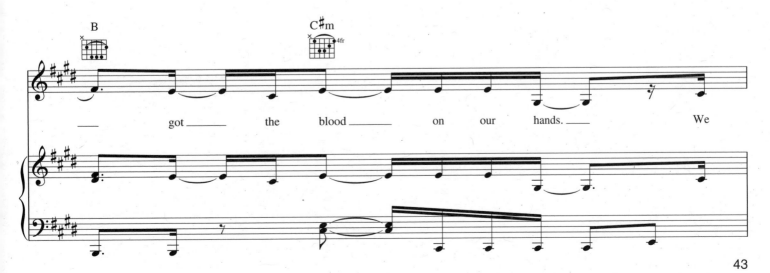

got the blood on our hands. We

on - ly re - ceive what we _____ de - mand; _____ and if

we want hell, _____ then hell's _____ what we'll have. _____

D.S. al Coda

Turn it a - round. _____

44

Drink the Water

Words and Music by
Jack Johnson

salt - y ____ sub - sti - tute, ___ just not a - go - in' to do. ___ I

need some __ air _____ if I'm a - go - in' to live __ through

the ex - pe - ri - ence. __ Re - minds me of ____ a clock that

just won't __ tick. _____ I want to wake __ up

from this - a con-cus-sion, _____ but my dream is just _____ not done. _____ I'm

late a - gain. _____ It's just one of those _____

bad days. Look out - side _____ and be care-ful what you ride. _____ You

just might _____ find _____ that you're out of time _____

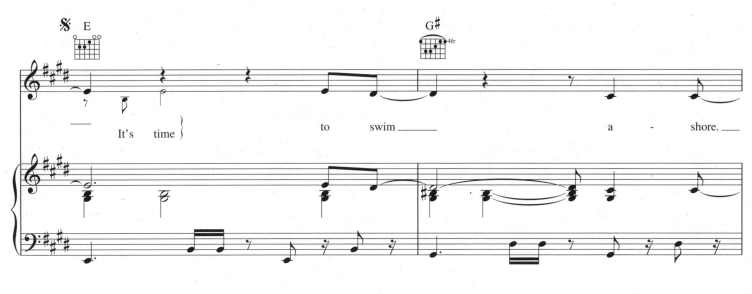

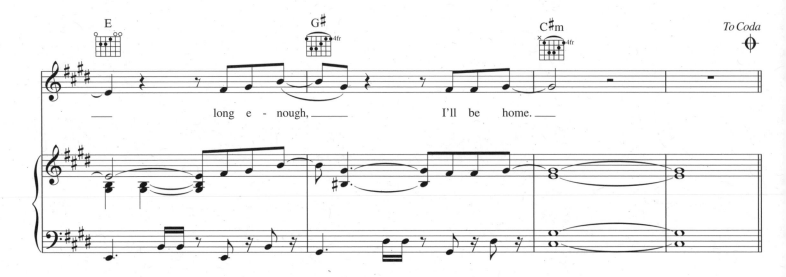

He's got de - lu - sions be - tween _____ his ears; _____ man, it takes _____

_____ up too _____ much space. _____

And all that ten - sion be - tween _____ his gears, _____ man, he'll nev -

er ev - er leave _____ this place. _____ He's got

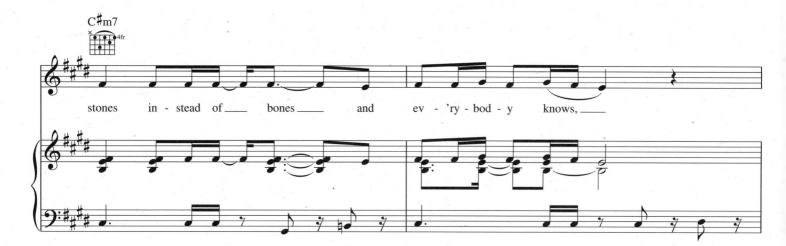

stones in - stead of _____ bones _____ and ev - 'ry - bod - y knows, _____

ah, _____ man, that can make _ you real, real _____ slow. _ And if

heav - en was _ be - low, he'd know just where to go.

50

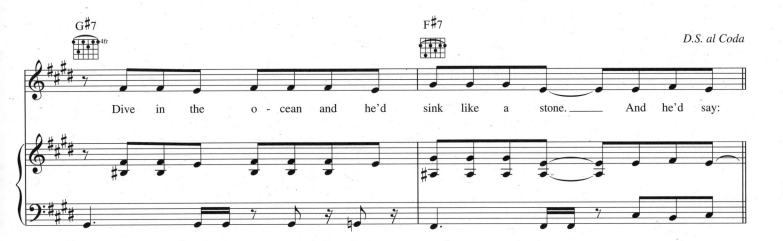

D.S. al Coda

Dive in the o - cean and he'd sink like a stone. ____ And he'd say:

Hold ____ on ____ if you can. ____ You're gon - na sink fast - er than you can i - mag -

ine, so hold. ____ Ah, just

hold ____ on ____ if you can. ____ You're gon - na sink fast - er than you can i - mag -

Fall Line

Words and Music by
Jack Johnson

and the ones that fill the frame. I turn it up, but then I turn it off be - cause I ___

___ can't stand ___ when they start to talk a - bout the hurt - ing and kill - ing. Whose shoes ___

___ are we fill - ing? The dam - age and ru - in, man, the things that we're do - ing. God,

we got - ta stop, we got - ta turn it all off; we got - ta re - wind,

start it up a- gain be-cause we fell a- cross___ the fall___ line.___

Ain't there noth-ing sa - cred an - y - more?___

Na, na, na,___ na, na,___ na, na, na.___

things that kept him want-ing more un-til he fi-n'lly reached the core. He

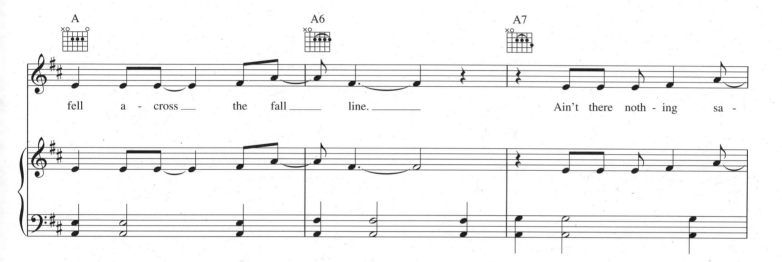

fell a-cross___ the fall___ line.___ Ain't there noth-ing sa-

cred an-y-more?___

Na, na, na,___ na, na,___ na, na, na.___

Flake

Words and Music by
Jack Johnson

Moderately

I know she said it's al - right, but you can make it up next time. _

I know she knows it's not _ right.

There ain't no use in ly - ing. May - be she thinks I know __

__ some - thing, may - be, may - be she thinks __ it's fine.

May - be she knows some - thing __ I don't. I'm so, __ I'm so ti - red,

I'm so tired of try - ing. It seems to me that "may - be," __

I would - n't want to break 'em, nah, I would - n't want to break 'em.

May - be she'll help me to un - tie _____ this, but un - til then, _____ well,

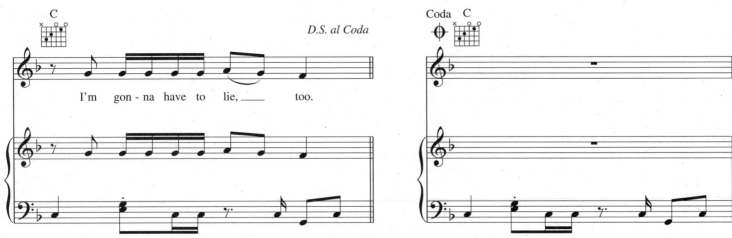

I'm gon - na have to lie, _____ too.

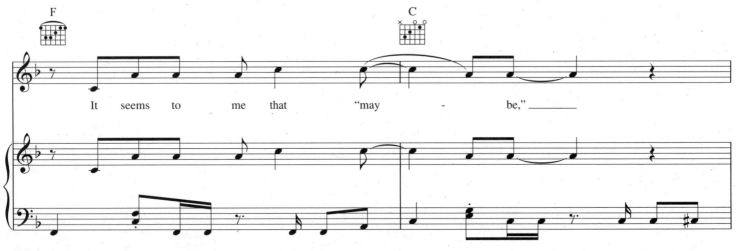

It seems to me that "may - be," _____

it pret - ty much al - ways means ___ "no." So don't ___

___ tell ___ me; ___ you might just let ___ it go. ___

mf

Fortunate Fool

Words and Music by
Jack Johnson

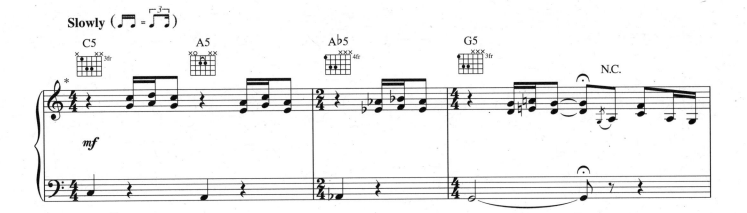

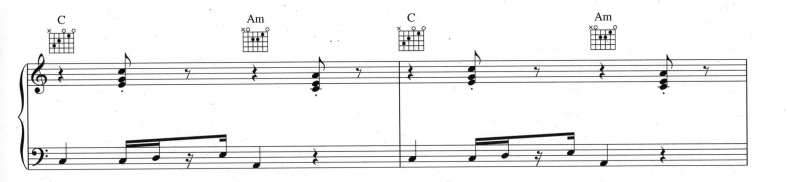

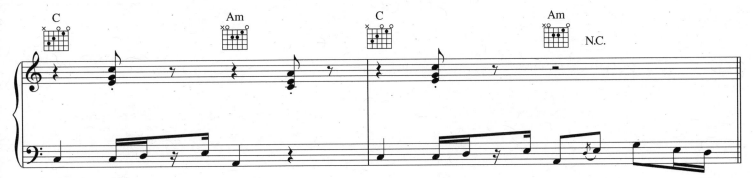

*Recorded a half step lower.

She's got it all _____ fig - ured out. ____
She knows the world _ is just _ her stage, _
She's got it all _____ fig - ured out. ____

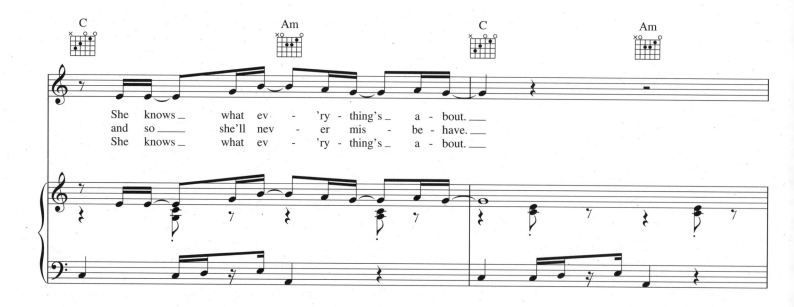

She knows _ what ev - 'ry - thing's _ a - bout. ____
and so ____ she'll nev - er mis - be - have. ____
She knows _ what ev - 'ry - thing's _ a - bout. ____

And when _ an - y - bod - y doubts _ her or sings songs _ with - out ____
She gives _ thanks for what _ they gave _ her; man, they prac - ti - c'lly made _
And when _ an - y - bod - y doubts _ her or sings songs _ a - bout _

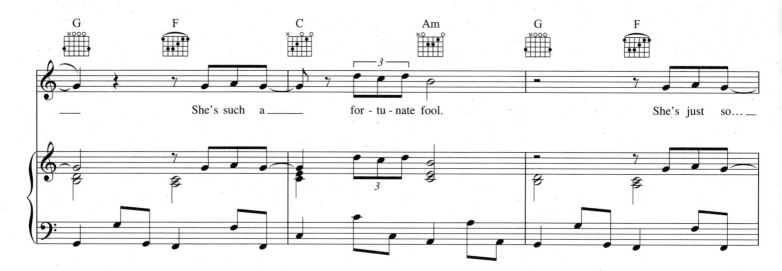

She's such a _____ for-tu-nate fool. She's just so..._____

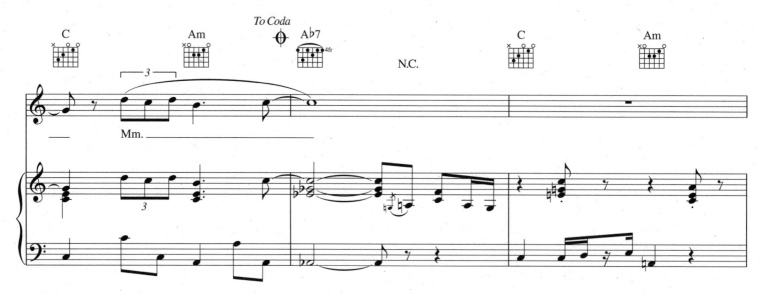

Mm. _____

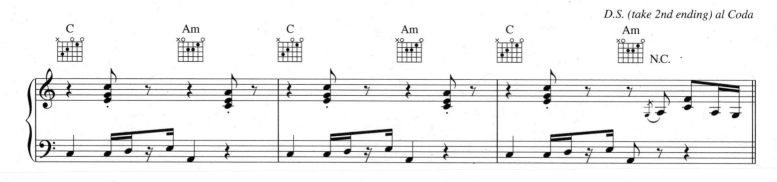

F-Stop Blues

Words and Music by
Jack Johnson

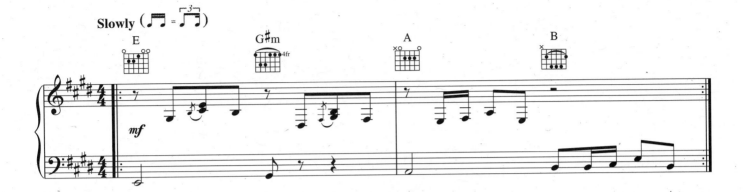

Her - mit crabs and cow - ry shells _ crush be - neath his feet _ as he comes _ towards you. _ He's

wav - ing at you. _____ Lift _____ him _____

up to see what you can see. ___ He be-gins his fo-cus-ing. ___ He's

aim - ing at you. _____ And now ___ he has ___

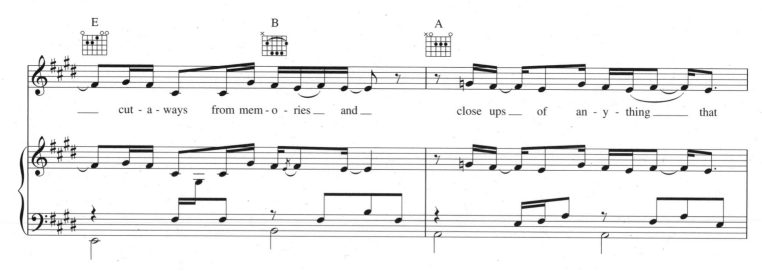

___ cut - a - ways from mem - o - ries ___ and ___ close ups ___ of an - y - thing _____ that

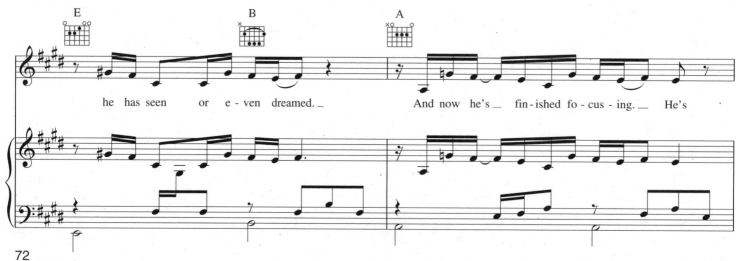

he has seen or e - ven dreamed. ___ And now he's ___ fin - ished fo - cus - ing. ___ He's

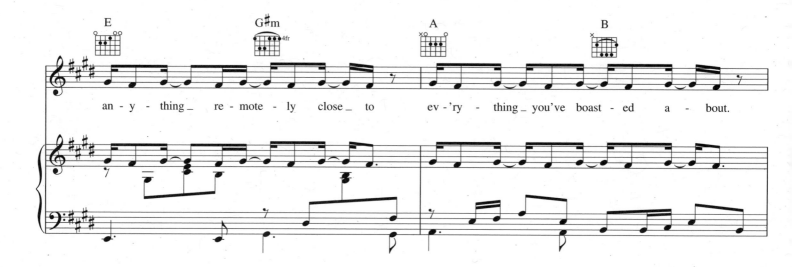

an-y-thing___ re-mote-ly close___ to ev-'ry-thing___ you've boast-ed a-bout.

Look who's cry-ing now.___

To Coda

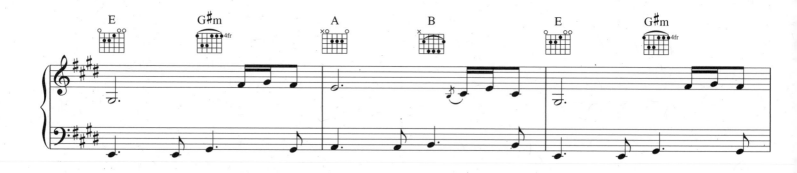

Drift-wood floats af-ter years of e-ro-sion.

In - com - ing tide __ touch - es roots to ex - pose them. Quick - sand __ steals my __ shoes. __

Clouds bring the f - stop blues. _____

D.S. al Coda

Coda

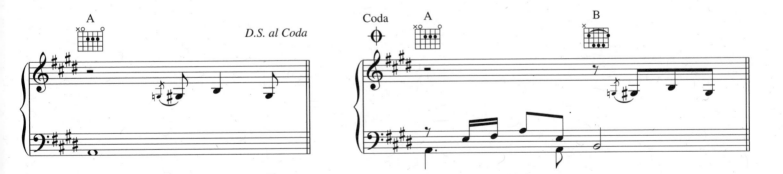

Repeat and fade

Good People

Words and Music by
Jack Johnson

*Recorded a half step lower.

D.S. al Coda I

Coda I

79

So far a - way, __ but I can feel the de - bris. Can you feel __ it?

You in - ter - rupt me from a friend - ly con - ver - sa - tion

to tell me how great __ it's all __ gon - na be. __

You might no - tice some hes - i - ta - tion 'cause

it's im-por-tant to you; __ it's not im-por-tant to me. __ Mm, mm, mm, mm.

Way down by the edge of your __ rea-son,

well, it's be-gin-ning to show, __ and all I real-ly wan-na know is where'd all the good peo-ple

D.S. al Coda II

Coda II

They got this and that with a rat-tle a tat. __ Test-ing, __
(Where'd all the good peo-ple go?) __

one, two. Man, what-cha gon-na do? Bad news, mis-used, give me some truth. _ You got

too much to lose. Who's _ side are we on to-day, _ an-y-way? _ O-kay, what-ev-er you say. _
(Where'd all the good peo-ple go?) _

Wrong or res-o-lute but in the mood to o-bey. _ Sta-tion to sta-tion, de-sen-si-

tiz-ing the na-tion. Go-ing, go-ing, gone.
(Where'd all the good peo-ple go?) _

Holes to Heaven

Words and Music by
Jack Johnson

Moderately slow

air was more than hu - man and __ the heat __ was more than hun - gry, and the cars __
Dis - em - bark - ing from __ the port __ with no __ mis - takes of an - y sort. Mov -

__ were square and spit - ting die - sel fumes. __
ing south, the en - gine run - ning smooth. __

The bulls were run-ning wi - ld be-cause they're
Of - fi - cials were quite friend - ly once we

big and mean _ and sa - cred, and the chil - dren were play-ing crick-et with _ no shoes. _
drowned them with _ our sweet _ talk and we bribed _ them with our cig - a - rettes _ and booze. _

The
The

next morn - ing we woke _ up, man, _ with a sev - en ho - ur drive. ____
next morn - ing we woke _ up, man, _ with the sun - rise to the right, ____

There we were___ stuck in ___ ⎱ Port Blaire,___ where boats break___ and chil - dren stare.___
mov - ing back___ north to ___ ⎰

There were so ___ man - y few - er ques - tions when ___ stars were still just the holes ___ to heav -

en.　　　　Mm,　　mm._____　　　　　　And

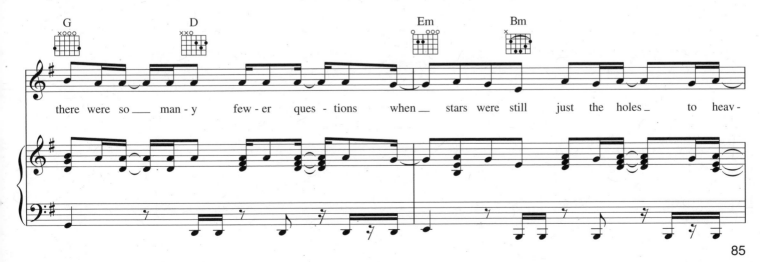

there were so ___ man - y few - er ques - tions when ___ stars were still just the holes ___ to heav -

Repeat and fade

The Horizon Has Been Defeated

Words and Music by
Jack Johnson

*Recorded a half step lower.

ri - zon has been de - feat - ed by the pi - rates of the new age. ___
Fu - ture com - pli - ca - tions in the strings be - tween the cans.
Thing - a - ma - jig - saw puz - zled; an - ger, don't you step too close.

But
'Cause

A - li - en ___ ca - si - nos, well, may - be it's just time to say ___ that
no prints can come from fin - gers if ma - chines be - come our hands. ___ And then the
peo - ple are lone - ly and on - ly an - i - mals with fan - cy shoes. ___ And

things can go ___ bad ___ and make you want to run a - way. ___ But
feet be - come ___ the ___ wheels, and then the wheels be - come the cars. ___ And then the
hal - le - lu - jah zig - zag noth - ing, and mis - er - y, it's on the loose. ___ 'Cause

To Coda

as we grow ___ old - er, the trou - ble just seems to
rigs be - gin ___ to ___ drill un - til the drill - ing goes too

stay.
far.

Things can go ___ bad ___ and make you want to run a - way. ___ But

as we grow ___ old - er, ho - ri - zon be - gins to

fade, fade, fade,

D.S. al Coda

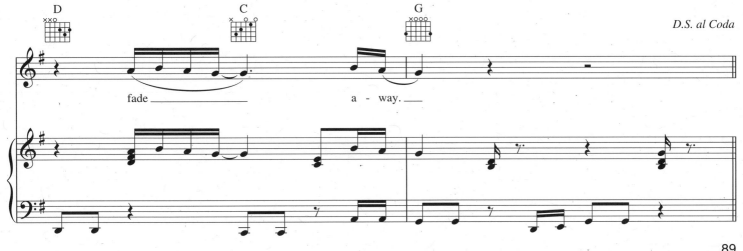

fade _____ a - way. ___

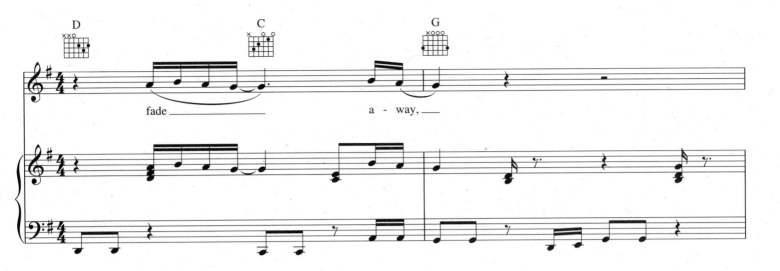

fade _____ a - way, ___

fade _____ a - way. ___

Fade,   fade,   fade. _____

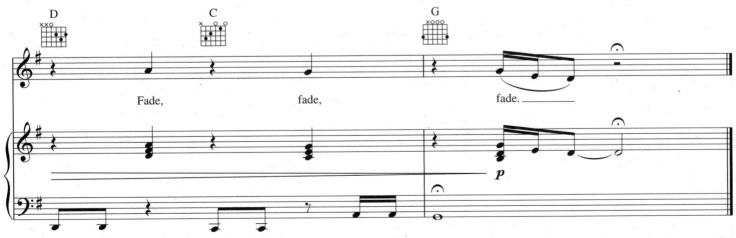

Fade,   fade,   fade. _____

Inaudible Melodies

Words and Music by
Jack Johnson

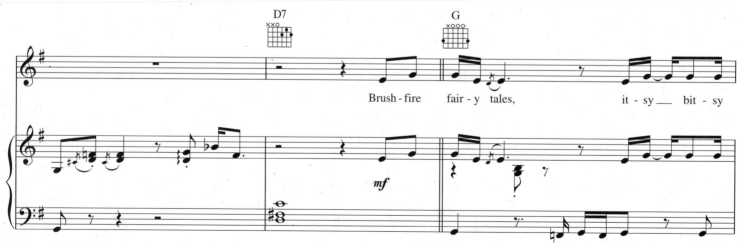

Brush - fire   fair - y   tales,   it - sy ___ bit - sy

*Recorded a half step lower.

plas - tic plants. __ Pret - ty pic - tures of things we ate; __ we are on - ly what __

__ we hate. But in the long run we have found __ si - lent __ films are

full of sound, __ in - au - di - bly free.

Slow __ down, ev - 'ry - one; __ you're mov - ing too fast. __

Frames can't catch you when you're mov-ing like _____ that.

Slow down, ev-'ry-one; _____ you're mov-ing too fast. _____

Frames can't catch you when you're mov-ing like _____ that, mov-ing _____ too...

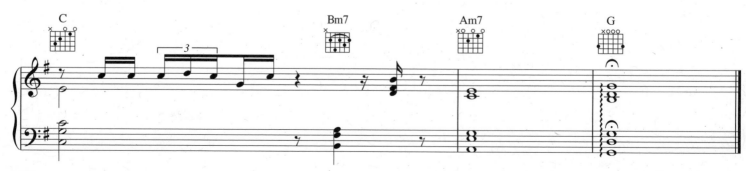

Middle Man

Words and Music by
Jack Johnson

May-be give a friend a call in-stead of mak-ing him con - fused.

What a ter-ri-ble thing _ for you _ to do.

What an aw - ful thing _ for you _ to say.

What a ter - ri - ble thing _ for you _ to re - lay.

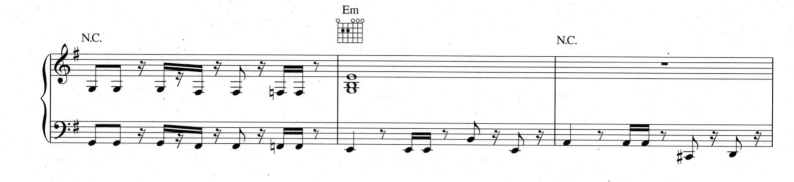

Well,

Con -

fused. _____
(Some-how we al - ways get stuck in the mid-dle.

What an aw - ful thing _ for you _ to do. _
Some-how we al - ways get stuck in the mid - dle.

Some-how we al - ways get stuck in the mid - dle.)

Con -

fused. _____
(Some-how we al - ways get stuck in the mid - dle.

What an aw - ful thing _ for you _ to say. _
Some-how we al - ways get stuck in the mid - dle.

Some-how we al - ways get stuck in the mid - dle.)

Mudfootball
(For Moe Lerner)

Words and Music by
Jack Johnson

Moderately fast

Sat - ur - day morn - ing and it's __ time to go. One day these could be the days, but who could have known? __
Sun - day morn - ing and it's __ time to go. Been rain - ing all night so ev - 'ry - bod - y knows.
Mon - day morn - ing and it's __ time to go. Wet trunks and school books and sand on my toes. __ Do

Load - ing in the back of a pick - up truck. Rid - ing with the boys and push - ing the luck.
O - ver to the field for tack - le foot - ball. Big hits, big hats, yeah, give me the ball.
an - y - thing you can to stop the bus - stop blues, like driv - ing a pa - did - dle with a burnt - out fuse. Well, my

Noth-ing's gon - na change, there's no ___ need to ___ com - plain. ___

D.S. al Coda

We used _ to laugh _ a lot, _ but on - ly be - cause _ we thought _ that ev -

'ry - thing good al - ways would, _ ev - 'ry - thing good . al - ways would _ re - main. _

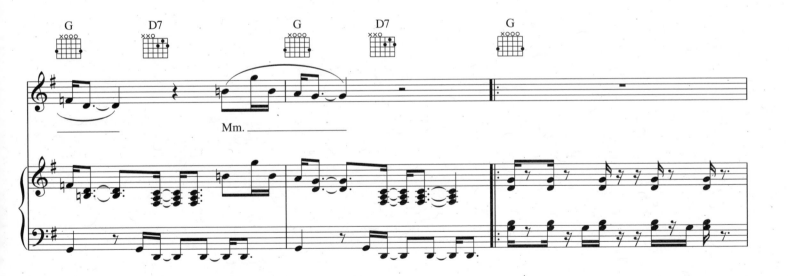

Mm. _

Repeat and fade

Posters

Words and Music by
Jack Johnson

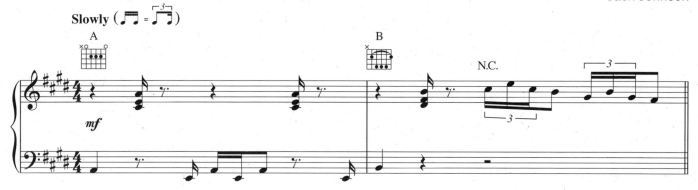

Look - ing at him - self but wish - ing he was some - one else be - cause the
Look - ing at her - self but wish - ing she was some - one else be - cause the

pos - ters on the wall they don't look like him at all. _____
bod - y of the doll, it don't look like hers at all. _____

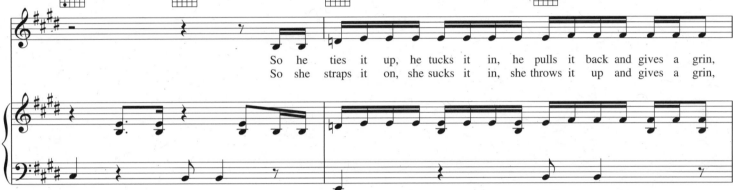

So he ties it up, he tucks it in, he pulls it back and gives a grin,
So she straps it on, she sucks it in, she throws it up and gives a grin,

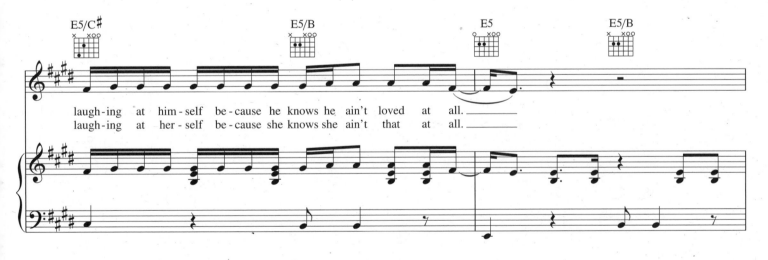

laugh - ing at him - self be - cause he knows he ain't loved at all. _____
laugh - ing at her - self be - cause she knows she ain't that at all. _____

He gets his cour - age from the can; it makes him feel like a man _ be - cause he's
All caught up in the trends, well, the truth be - gan to bend, and the

lov - ing all the la - dies but the la - dies don't love him at all. _____
next thing you know, man, there just ain't no truth left at all. _____

'Cause when he's not drunk, he's on - ly stuck on him - self, ___ and then _
'Cause when the pret - ty girl walks, she walks so proud. _ And when the

_____ he has the nerve to say ___ he needs a de - cent girl. _____
pret - ty girl laughs, oh, man, _ she laughs so loud. _____

And if it ain't this, then it's that. As a mat-ter of fact, ___

___ she has-n't had ___ a day ___ to re - lax since she's ___ lost her ___

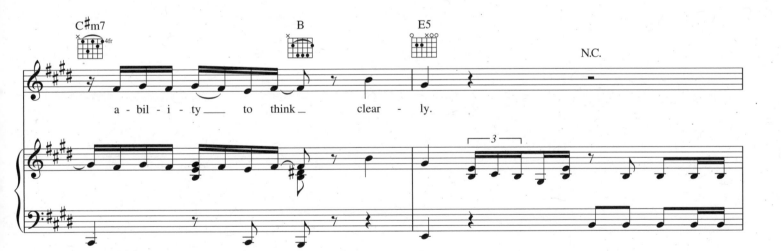

a - bil - i - ty ___ to think ___ clear - ly.

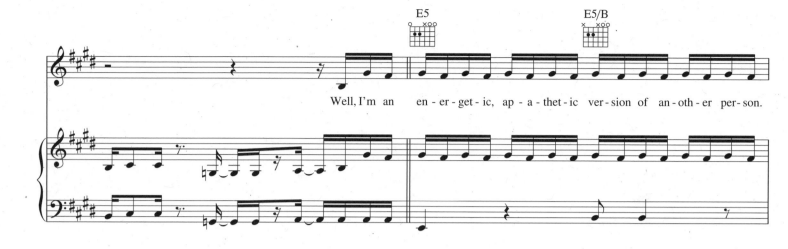

Well, I'm an en-er-get-ic, ap-a-thet-ic ver-sion of an-oth-er per-son.

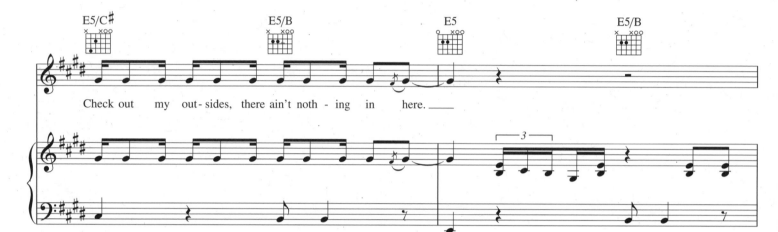

Check out my out-sides, there ain't noth-ing in here. ____

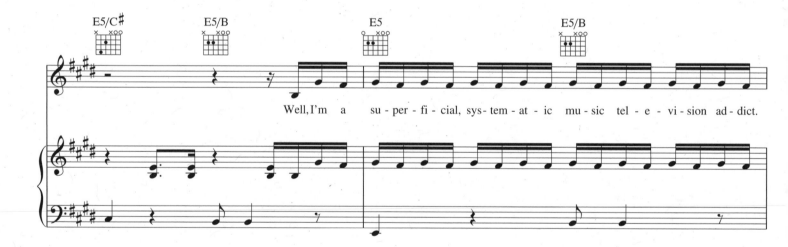

Well, I'm a su-per-fi-cial, sys-tem-at-ic mu-sic tel-e-vi-sion ad-dict.

Check out my out-sides; there ain't noth-ing in... Here ____ comes an-oth-er one just ____ like the oth-er one.

Sitting, Waiting, Wishing

Words and Music by
Jack Johnson

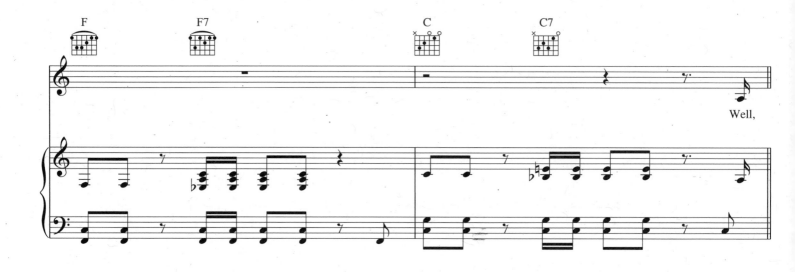

I was sit - ting, wait - ing, wish - ing you be - lieved __ in su - per - sti - tions;
sang your songs, I danced your dance; I gave your friends __ all a chance.
if I was in your po - si - tion, I'd put down all __ my am - mu - ni - tion. I'd

Just sit - ting, wait - ing. ___

Just wait a min - ute. ___

Just sit - ting, wait - ing. ___

D.S. al Coda

Well,

118

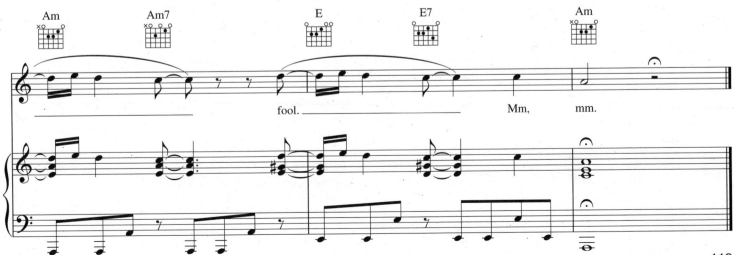

Staple It Together

Lyrics by
Jack Johnson

Music by
Jack Johnson and Merlo Podlewski

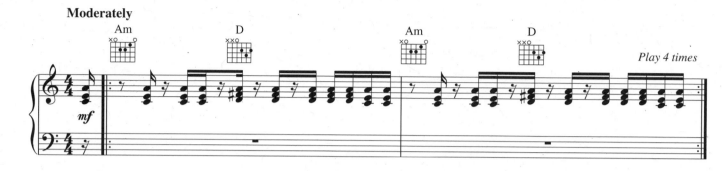

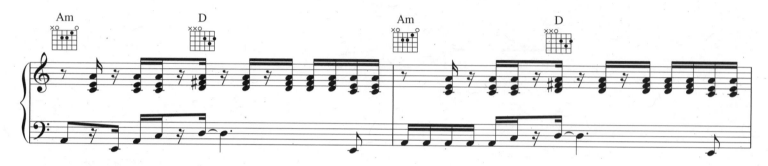

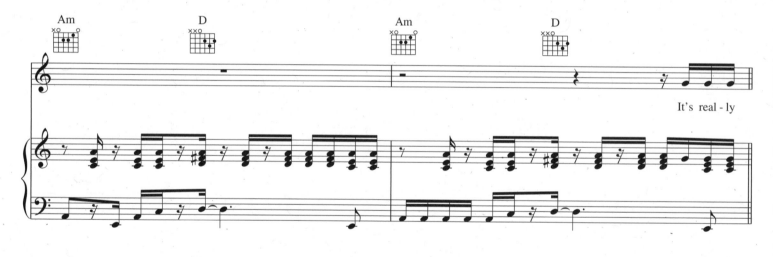

too bad.
guess you could say
He be-came a pris-'ner of his own past.
that he don't e-ven know where to be-gin.
He stabbed a mo-
'Cause he looked

It's real-ly

ment in the back with a round thumb-tack that held ___ up the list of things ___ he got to do. It's real-ly
___ both ways but he was so a-fraid dig-gin' deep in-to the ditch ev-'ry chance he missed and the mess

Am   D   Am   D

no good.   He's mov-ing on ___ be-fore he un - der - stood. ___ He shot the fu-
he made.   'Cause hate ___ is such a strong word. ___ And ev-'ry brick ___

Am   D   Am   D

ture in the foot with ev-'ry step he took, _ ah, from the plac-es that he'd been 'cause he for-got to look. } Bet-ter
___ he laid a mis-take. They say ___ that his walls are get-tin' tall - er, this world is get-ting small-er.

It's real - ly

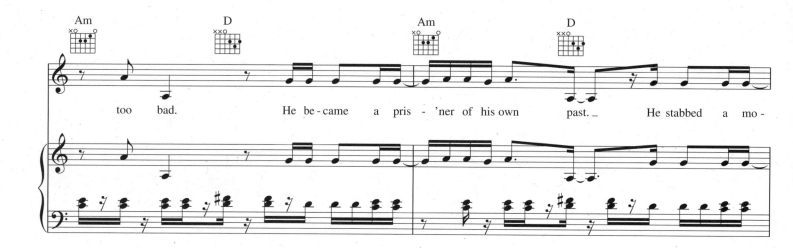

too bad. He be-came a pris-'ner of his own past._ He stabbed a mo-

D.S. (lyric 1) al Coda

ment in the back with a round thumb-tack that held_ up the list of things_ he got to do. It's real-ly

Coda

Sta-ple it to-geth-er and call_ it bad weath-er. If the weath-er gets bet-ter, we should get to-geth-er.

Spend a lit-tle time or we could do what-ev-er. And if we get to-geth-er we'd be twice as clev-er. So

sta - ple it to - geth - er and call ___ it bad weath - er. Mm, mm. _____

Taylor

Words and Music by
Jack Johnson

They   say

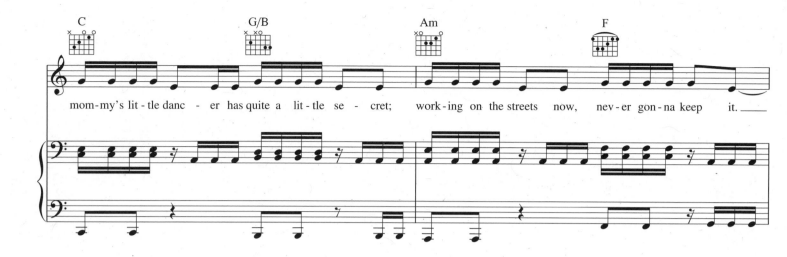

mom-my's lit-tle danc - er has quite a lit-tle se - cret; work-ing on the streets now, nev-er gon-na keep it. ___

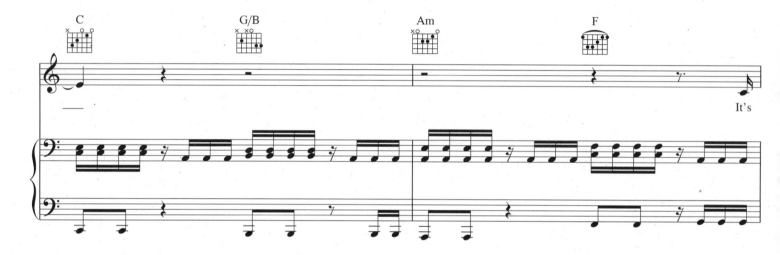

___ It's

quite an im-po-si - tion and now she's on - ly wish - ing that ___ she would have lis - tened to the words _ they said. _

___ Poor Tay - lor.

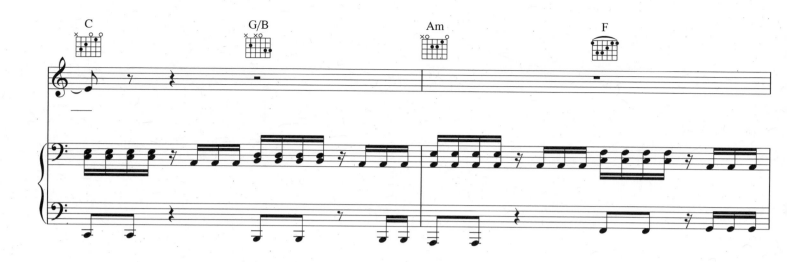

Pe - ter Pat - rick pit - ter pat - ters on the win - dow, but

Sun - ny Sil - hou - ette won't let him _____ in.

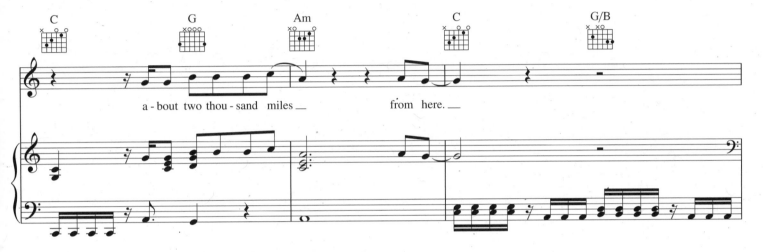

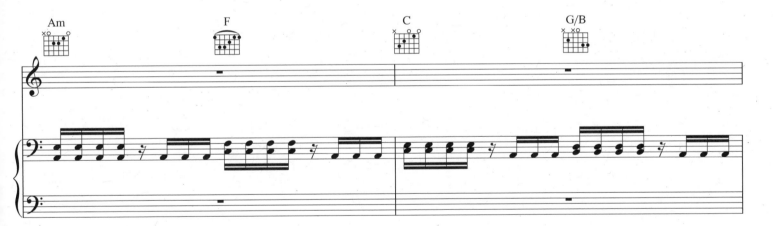

ing what she got - ta give___ to get a dol - lar bill.___

Used to be ___ a lim - ber chick - en, times___ a been a tick - ing. Now,___

___ she's fin - ger lick - ing to the man___ with the mon - ey in his pock - et, fly - ing in his rock - et, on-

ly stop - ping by on his way to a bet - ter world.___

If Tay - lor finds a bet - ter world, ___

then Tay - lor's gon - na run a - way. ___

A little slower

Times Like These

Words and Music by
Jack Johnson

And it al - ways goes on and on ___ and on and on and on.

On and on ___ and on and on and on it goes. ___ Mm, ___ hmm,

hmm. Mm, ___ hmm, hmm. ___ Mm; ___ hmm,

hmm. And there's al - ways been laugh - ing, cry - ing, birth and dy - ing, boys and girls ___

with hearts that take and give and break _ and heal and grow _ and re - cre - ate and raise _ and nur-

ture, but then hurt from time _ to times like _ these and times _ like _

_ those. What will be _ will be, _____ and so _ it goes. _

And there will al - ways be stop and go _ and fast and slow and ac - tion, re -

138

and on and on and on and on ___ it goes. ___ Mm, ___ hmm,

hmm. Mm, ___ hmm, hmm. ___ Mm, ___ hmm,

hmm. But some- how I ___ know it won't be the

same. Some- how I ___ know, nev- er be the same.

Traffic in the Sky

Words and Music by
Jack Johnson

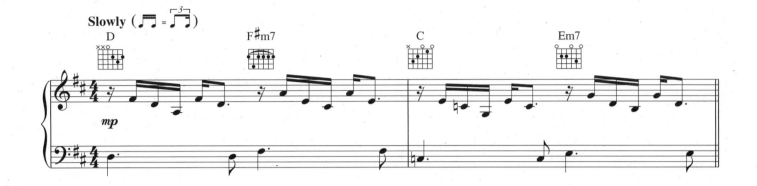

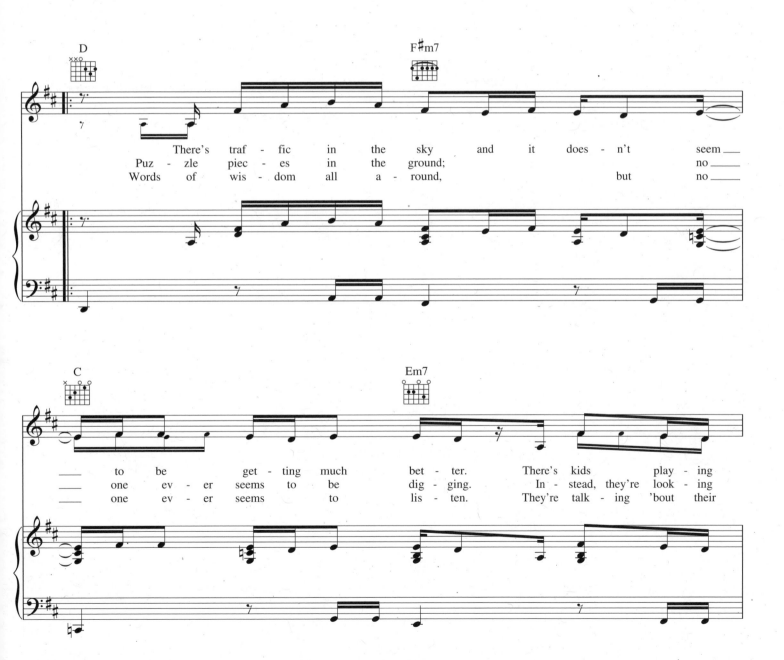

There's traf - fic in the sky and it does - n't seem ___ ___ to be get - ting much bet - ter. There's kids play - ing

Puz - zle piec - es in the ground; no ___ ___ one ev - er seems to be dig - ging. In - stead, they're look - ing

Words of wis - dom all a - round, but no ___ ___ one ev - er seems to lis - ten. They're talk - ing 'bout their

games	on	the	pave - ment,	draw - ing	waves	on	the	pave - ment,	mm,	hmm;
up	towards	the	heav - ens	with	their	eyes	on	the	heav - ens,	mm,	hmm;
plans	on	the	pa - per,	build - ing	up	from	the	pave - ment,	mm,	hmm;

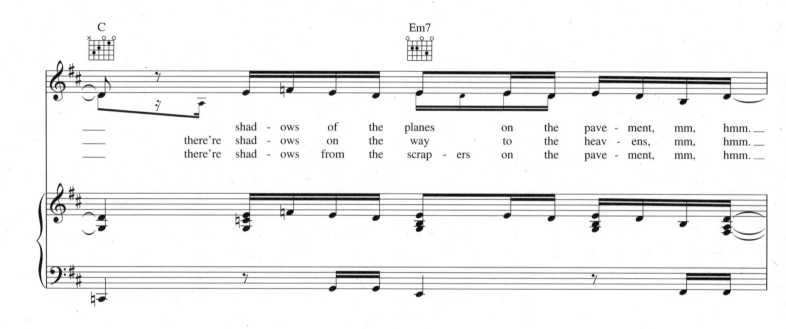

____		shad - ows	of	the	planes		on	the	pave - ment,	mm,	hmm.
____	there're	shad - ows	on	the	way		to	the	heav - ens,	mm,	hmm.
____	there're	shad - ows	from	the	scrap - ers		on	the	pave - ment,	mm,	hmm.

____	It's	e - nough	to	make	me	cry,	but	that	don't
____	It's	e - nough	to	make	me	cry,	but	that	don't
____	It's	e - nough	to	make	me	sigh,	but	that	don't

seem like it would make it feel bet - ter. May - be it's a
seem like it would make -it feel bet - ter. The an - swers could be
seem like it would make it feel bet - ter. The words are all a -

dream and if I scream, it will burst at the seams; ___ whole ___
found; we could learn from dig - ging down, but no _____
round, but the words are on - ly sounds, and no _____

___ place would fall in - to piec - es and then they'd
___ one ev - er seems to be dig - ging. In - stead, they'll
___ one ev - er seems to lis - ten. In - stead, they'll